Taking the Lead with Kindness

How to impact the world with fewer words and more action

Donald Clarke, Jr.

Copyediting and typesetting: Sally Hanan of Inksnatcher.com
Cover design: Daniel Roman of Roman Ink

Ordering Information: Special discounts are available on quantity purchases by corporations, associations, and others. For details, contact the author at the email address above.

Taking the Lead with Kindness: How to impact the world with fewer words and more action/Donald Clarke, Jr.

ISBN: 9798743321919

*To my greatest church on the planet
that I have the honor and privilege to
serve bar none, you all are the
irreplaceable. This dream has come
alive because of all of you. I love you
all to life.*

Contents

Acknowledgments

I WOULD LIKE TO give an acknowledgement to my Savior and Lord, Jesus Christ, who has made all things possible in my life. Without him I would be nothing.

Secondly, I want to acknowledge my family, who have always believed in me and always encouraged me to reach my full potential, never accepting the status quo.

To my son—my rock and my joy. Thank you for being one of the greatest gifts a father could receive. If Dad did it, you can too.

Introduction

I FIND IT STRANGE that I would be authoring a book on kindness because I think that being kind, especially to another human being, should be as automatic as our need for water. However, I've discovered that, in our new normal of social media, many people are not kind, nor are they forgiving—especially pertaining to individuals in the public eye, i.e., politicians, pastors, actors, or CEOs who have fallen from grace. The climate of the culture has become cynical. Nice gestures have been overtaken with people searching for the hidden motive behind such an expression. People are more concerned with looking out for themselves than others.

In this book, I'll be talking about ways we can impact our spheres of influence via viable acts of kindness. I will present key concepts on how to maintain a positive attitude and how to exude kindness, even with people who are indifferent to us. Finally, I'll demonstrate the effectiveness of kindness, even in hostile environments!

I am the lead pastor of Harvest Fire in Miami Gardens, Florida—a church founded by my parents, Donald Sr. and Helga Clarke. They faithfully served there for forty years before the torch was passed to me! None of this would have transpired if someone had not been kind to my father. That one act changed everything for hundreds of people. I'll talk about that too.

Kindness is not a weakness! Kindness is an attribute of leaders who want to influence and change the world for the better. There is an old Western Caribbean adage that states that a little encouragement sweetens the labor. Good character begins with kindness, and I believe it should also end with kindness.

Donald Clarke, Jr.

CHAPTER 1

KINDNESS: THE LOST ART

*The islanders showed us
unusual kindness. They built a
fire and welcomed us all
because it was raining and
cold.*
—Acts 28:2

Jesus showed kindness in many ways. We can too. The kind acts we do for people might help them financially, physically, emotionally, or spiritually. What we do depends on what they need and what we know God is telling us to do. I am a Christian before I am a pastor, and I use the Word of God as my compass to navigate through life, help me make good decisions, and live according to how God expects me to live on a daily basis. When he says "Clothe yourselves with compassion, kindness, humility, gentleness and patience" (Colossians 3:12), that needs to become part of my character. That's how I need to live.

The Principle of Kindness

Kindness is a fruit of the Spirit. "The fruit of the Spirit is love, joy, peace, forbearance, kindness, goodness, faithfulness, gentleness and self-control" (Galatians 5:22–23). Like a fig tree should produce figs in season, we should produce love, joy, peace, forbearance, kindness, goodness, faithfulness, gentleness, and self-control all the time. It should be our response to everything and everyone.

> *There is no man whose kindness we may not sometime want.*
> *—Noah Webster*

Giving to Get

We all like incentives, right? When I started my freshman year of college, I worked as a luggage salesman at a part-time gig. I was driven by the commission I could earn if I could successfully make a sale on an expensive, top-of-the-line luggage set. Sales is still one of the highest-paid industries one can be involved in because the ability to earn commissions is based on what you sell. You work for it, therefore you earn it. However, with kindness, there is no incentive one can work for.

We all want to experience the kindness of others in our times of need, but we can't show kindness today just so we'll get kindness in return tomorrow. Jesus was speaking to his disciples when he said "In everything, do to others what you would have them do to you" (Matthew 7:12). This particular phrase is known as the Golden Rule, implying that when we do good to others, the favor will be returned to us like good karma. That is right, but only to an extent! Jesus was attempting to teach his disciples that exhibiting kindness should not be for a benefit such as self-recognition but to esteem another person over ourselves. It's more a principle of selflessness—doing something purely for another person's benefit and getting no personal benefit from it.

True character is when you do something nice for someone who doesn't have the resources or ability to help you back! The point I am making is that the Golden Rule should never be based on what we can receive back but more on what we can show instead! The truth of the matter is that when we show kindness to others, God rules in justice and will give us the recompense for our sacrifice of love, whether or not the person we show kindness to returns the favor or not.

Belittling Kindness

I see cynicism toward those who show kindness to others. Like the old adage that chivalry is dead, people only expect others to display kindness if it will be reciprocated! If someone is kind, the questions that lie in the depth of the receiver's subconsciousness are: *What is the hidden motive or reason why they are showing this act of concern toward me? What do they want from me? This is too good to be true. Why is this person overextending themselves, placing their needs on the backburner?* To some extent, there is a disbelief that there are individuals who are willing to not just assist us when we are in need but are also willing to go the extra mile for us.

Looking After Number One

We now live in the new normal of the social media age, where the whole purpose of these mediums or platforms is to promote our best selfies, accomplishments, possessions, or relationships. While I am totally for this medium and am an avid user, it centers itself around what my father used to express as "me, myself, and I syndrome," or as "the ungodly trinity!" Our culture today is so engulfed and even hammered with phrases of self-care, self-preservation, and self-promotion that it distorts our perspective on helping others around us. Most people seek the return, and if one isn't promised, they see no reason to engage in assisting a person who desperately needs their act of kindness.

The world is built on the "what have you done for me lately" syndrome, where most people will do only what you do for them. In the kingdom of God, this is reversed. We do for others what we hope they would do for us should we ever be in a predicament needing help—we hope they would express kindness without ever looking for a return.

The Pharisees were very aware of what they would and would not benefit from. They had plenty of rules about what they supposed God wanted, but then said, for example, that any money that could be used to help a person's parents should go to them instead (Matthew 15:4–6). They perverted kindness while Jesus came to embody it. He expects the same of us.

CHAPTER 2

ACTS OF KINDNESS

*The next day we landed at
Sidon; and Julius, in kindness
to Paul, allowed him to go to
his friends so they might
provide for his needs.*
—Acts 27:2–4

Anything that physically shows we care about what someone else needs or is going through is considered an act of kindness. Kindness is showing the love of Jesus to people whose only chance of seeing Jesus is through us! Many people will dismiss what we say but want to see what we will do for them in a time of need. Theodore Roosevelt said it this way: "No one cares how much you know until they know how much you care." We can impact our world by saying a lot less and doing a lot more for others.

We can show kindness in so many ways—buying groceries or meals; paying off medical bills, debts, or utility bills; driving people to their appointments or to church; praying; showing mercy and forgiveness; doing handyman jobs; helping with taxes; teaching job skills. The list is endless.

The Crowd Got Hungry

I just need to park here for a moment to express how happy I am that God never sits so high that he is not concerned with the needs of humanity. Not only is God concerned about us, but he cares and he provides when we are hungry!

In Matthew 14:13–21, we see Jesus's compassion for the hungry masses. Crowds of people, thousands, followed Jesus to hear him teach and perform great miracles. There came a point when the crowd got hungry and needed something to eat. Jesus told his disciples that they needed to feed the people. His disciples told him that they lacked the resources, but then a boy came up to them with a basket of five loaves of bread and two fish. Jesus took what the boy had, blessed it, and performed one of the greatest miracles and mysteries of all time—he multiplied the five loaves of bread and two fish into enough to feed the masses of people, himself, and the disciples with leftovers to spare. Don't ask me how this was done! I could never mathematically figure it out. It is mind-blowing, impossible, and unbelievable, yet miraculous all at the same time. He was able to consider the needs of the people and focus on that more than his message. Jesus had the ability to see the needs of others, have compassion on their plight, and meet their needs via his act of kindness! Ingeniously, he was able to get their attention spiritually because he catered to their physical need first.

I can only imagine how exhausted Jesus was going from town to town, teaching, performing miracles, and ministering to his disciples. After teaching and then hearing about his cousin's murder at Herod's hands (John 14:1–12), Jesus could have said, "Well, folks, I'm tired and my disciples need my attention at this time, so we are going to retreat to private quarters," but he didn't. He even did this a second time, feeding four thousand people with seven loaves and a few small fish (Mark 8:1–9).

As Carl Buehner said, people will forget what you said, people will forget what you did, but people will never forget how you made them feel. Jesus lived demonstrating such kindness that people have never forgotten.

She Just Wanted Something to Eat

There was a story some time ago, which made headlines on national news, of a lady who was shoplifting grocery items from Whole Foods (of all places). The reason I say that is because you and I know that shopping at Whole Foods is extremely expensive. You can round up ten items in your grocery basket and it could cost you anywhere from seventy to eighty dollars, easily. I might be exaggerating just a little, but shopping at Whole Foods is not as economical as paying your friendly Target or Walmart prices.

This woman stuffed all the items in her dress, and the store manager alerted the police to what was going on. As soon as they saw her about to proceed out the door, they stopped her. The three policemen asked the lady if everything was okay. She replied yes. They asked if they could search her because they were notified that she was shoplifting. When they made that statement, she cried profusely and gave them all the items she'd tried to steal. One of the officers asked her what was going on. She replied that she was hungry and just wanted something to eat. She had lost her job and didn't know where to go or what to do next. Instead of arresting this woman and taking her in, the three policemen decided to pool their monies together to purchase the items the woman needed to help her in her time of need. The woman was overwhelmed with gratitude and cried uncontrollably as she thanked the officers for their kind gesture.

I tell this story to show that the acts of kindness we show can change our world for the better. While I understand there are people who are bent on milking the system and taking advantage of good people, I personally believe that the majority of people want to do better, and every now and then we get to offer a little hand up to those in need of it!

The Unexpected Kindness of Strangers

Reader's Digest asked people who had experienced the unexpected kindness of strangers to submit their stories. The stories are powerful..[1]

> I forgot about the rules on liquids in carry-on luggage, so when I hit security at the airport, I had to give up all my painting supplies. When I returned a week later, an attendant was at the baggage area with my paints. Not only had he kept them for me, but he'd looked up my return date and time in order to meet me.
>
> —Marilyn Kinsella, Canmore, Canada
>
> My neighbors have been the best since we moved in. When my husband got brain cancer, they helped with yard work and snow removal. When Jim passed away, they were always helping me, anything they could. Meals, yard work, snow removal, putting my

---

[1] https://www.rd.com/article/kindness-strangers/

trashcan away when I would forget. They still continue to care for me and if they don't see me outside in a while, they text to make sure I am alright and not down or anything.

—Shelly Golay, Casper, Wyoming

As I left a party, I got on the wrong freeway and was immediately lost. I pulled over to the shoulder and called my roadside-assistance provider. She tried to connect me to the California Highway Patrol, but that call never went through. Hearing the panic in my voice, she came up with a plan B: "You're near this office," she said. "I'm about to go off shift. Stay put, and I'll find you." Ten minutes later, she rolled up. She guided me not only to the right freeway but all the way to the correct freeway exit.

—Michelle Arnold, Santee, California

All three stories above show us what kindness looks like—caring, practical help, compassion, and comfort. The world needs Jesus, and if we are to be his representatives, that means everyone needs our kindness and acts of kindness so they can see his love in action!

Kindness in a Pandemic

At the time of this writing, COVID–19, otherwise known as a coronavirus, has essentially brought the world to its knees. We have seen more deaths in America from this than Vietnam, Pearl Harbor, and 9/11 combined. COVID–19 has devastated families, businesses, and livelihoods, and it has changed how we interact with one another. We now have social distancing and avoid mass gatherings due to rules recommended by the Centers for Disease Control and Prevention. The world has been restricted and lives altered. People are left living on edge as everyone is paranoid of the person(s) they come in contact with, fearing they could be the next victim of this potentially deadly disease. Being quarantined has taken its toll on everyone's mental health. Yet amid all the uncertainty in this pandemic, individuals have found ways to be thoughtful toward others.

- One man living in an apartment complex put out a rack of supplies from his store for residents to take what they needed at no cost (including coveted toilet tissue that was out of stock the first few weeks of this global crisis).

- A boy played his drums outdoors for his neighbors, and his neighbors joined in with their pots and pans and any instrument they had. Together they created a musically fun experience in their own front yards.

- A group of young people, who took all the safety precautions, went to a senior adult daycare facility to sing songs, talk, and play games with the elderly who were shut in.

At the pinnacle of the pandemic, the church I pastor—Harvest Fire—was one of the first organizations to reopen its food pantry. By continuing food bank assistance, we helped single mothers and families whose jobs were furloughed in their desperate time of need. We took precautions following the guidelines of the Centers for Disease Control and Prevention (CDC), but it was a risk for all our volunteers; however, we chose to let kindness take the lead and not our fears.

The gestures of kindness were endless, but the effects were real. The world might have been in a crisis and resources may have been strained, but that was the time for the cream to rise to the top, for good people to stand and make a difference by actions, not words.

When to Show Kindness

Edmund Burke said "The only thing necessary for the triumph of evil is for good men to do nothing." Every day we have a choice to impact someone else. Perhaps the one person we touch will pass on the favor to another person, starting a domino effect. Before we know it, that one life we touched has touched many other lives, leaving a larger impact on the world. It all first begins with the willingness to extend ourselves to others.

Jesus shared with his disciples the importance of remembering the destitute of society (Matthew 25:35–40). He said, "I was hungry and you gave me something to eat, I was thirsty and you gave me something to drink, I was a stranger and you invited me in, I needed clothes and you clothed me, I was sick and you looked after me, I was in prison and you came to visit me" (vv. 35–36). The message Jesus taught the disciples in this message is: no matter what title you wear, how many degrees you obtain, how many accolades you receive, or how gifted you know you are, if you can't help those around you who are in need of assistance, it is as if you have rejected Jesus. "Truly I tell you, whatever you did for one of the least of these brothers and sisters of mine, you did for me" (v. 40).

If we are truly followers of Christ, if we profess Jesus as Lord of our lives and ruler of our hearts, then our actions should follow suit. We should be known by the kindness we display to others around us. Kindness and Christianity are parallel to one another. We cannot divorce one from the other. To be a Christian is to be kind, and to be kind is a direct reflection of our walk with Christ.

Showing kindness is not always about monetary gifts or resources, it's also the thought of caring enough for others around us that we are willing to do whatever is necessary to make their day better. It means taking the time to listen to an elderly person in a nursing home, extending our wisdom to an at-risk young man or woman, or simply helping distribute food at our local food bank. Those things can and will impact someone for the better.

> Happiness is the new rich.
> Inner peace is the new success.
> Health is the new wealth.
> Kindness is the new cool.
> —Syed Balkhi

My father used to say a person can catch more flies with honey than vinegar. Kindness has a magnetic attraction that compels people to want to be around you, learn from you, and mimic you. Cash may be king, but kindness is golden. Let's spread a little more kindness each and every day.

CHAPTER 3

How to Be Kind to Indifferent Individuals

*Love your enemies, do good to
them, and lend to them
without expecting to get
anything back. Then your
reward will be great, and you
will be children of the Most
High, because he is kind to the
ungrateful and wicked.*
—Luke 6:35

Truth be told, it's hard to express
kindness to some individuals—to
others who are indifferent to you.
Instead of giving you my opinion, though, I
want to talk to you about kingdom

principles on showing kindness to every person, no matter how you feel about them.

Principle 1: We have to clothe ourselves with kindness every day.

Kindness is a principle of the kingdom. Paul told us to "clothe [ourselves] with compassion, kindness, humility, gentleness and patience" (Colossians 3:12). You may ask me how in the world you can place kindness. Kindness is not like clothes I can put on my body; it is a characteristic, and that is an intangible. I believe Paul was referring to placing the characteristics of kindness as our first response to difficult people rather than our emotions.

Principle 2: Kindness is an act, not a feeling.

We can't only be kind to the people we like. Jesus said, "if you do good to those who are good to you, what credit is that to you? Even sinners do that" (Luke 6:33).

You've heard it said before that some people wear their feelings on their sleeve. That used to be me. If an egregious act was done to me, it was hard to get over the hump of my feelings. I wore it in my expressions, which could be easily observed by others. Anyone could tell when I wasn't a happy camper—from a previous incident that occurred—the minute they noticed me. It was even harder to show kindness to the offender of the crime, the one who had done me wrong, until I discovered that forgiveness and kindness are never about my emotions. Kindness is a kingdom principle.

Regardless of a person's chronological age, human beings can be petty and small when slighted. I have seen fights break out not just among teenagers who have a history of contention between them, but also among senior citizens who can't forgive each other and refuse to relinquish their ground or choose kindness. I have a coworker who is on my case like white on rice, and I am about to catch a case and tell them a few things! I need Jesus's help on this as much as anyone.

We need to love like Jesus. Now you may ask what love has to do with this. You might say that the people around you don't know what you are dealing with— your spouse, children, siblings, in-laws, or church family. Yes, they may not fully know or understand the depth of the dilemma of your pain, but I am trying to show that how we respond to the people in our lives who are challenging can eventually shift the temperature of that relationship, *if* you can consistently be kind, despite their response. Kill them with kindness.

Again, kindness is about exhibiting grace and is not based on how you feel. Feelings are suspect. We can't trust them. We know we love our spouse, but after a big argument, we might not be able to stand the sight of them for a few hours. Am I right or am I right? What I am saying is that feelings should never be a measure for how we treat others, even if they are not doing right by us.

Now I am not insinuating you should continually show kindness to someone who is abusive, belittling, or condescending to who you are as a person. You are not a punching bag, and you should never tolerate anyone treating you that way.

Principle 3: Kindness is a kingdom principle rooted in grace.

The most quoted and memorized scripture of all time, held up by fans at stadiums and at little league soccer, is John 3:16: "God so loved the world that he gave his one and only Son, that whoever believes in him shall not perish but have eternal life." If anyone had a reason to not show kindness or exhibit grace to humanity, it was God, yet he does so every day.

Humanity had it made in the garden of Eden. We had full autonomy in naming the animals; we had the authority to rule and dominate; and we only had to do one thing—obey God by not eating the fruit of the Tree of Knowledge of Good and Evil. I say "we" because when Adam and Eve fell, all of humanity fell, and that fall brought sin into the equation: death, disease, famine, pain, murder—you name it, it all came into play. God chose to undo what we brought in by sending his Son, Jesus Christ, the point of redemption and hope for mankind. Why do I mention all of this? Well, God did not have to send his only Son. He was not obligated to do so, but he did it to show how much he loved us and how he was willing to bankrupt heaven for our sake. He did it even though we were ungrateful, indifferent, and rebellious. This was the ultimate act of selfless love and kindness.

How many of us would offer our child as a sacrifice for the sins of others? You are probably saying "It's just not happening, Pastor!" God did just that and demonstrated to humanity firsthand what it is to show kindness to a world in which only a percentage of people will actually receive Jesus. A world in which many will reject him! God did not send his sacrifice based on how he felt, and thank God for that. He did it because he loved us, and love requires an action of kindness.

Showing kindness in a loveless marriage—where one spouse is not necessarily reciprocating kindness—is a tall order, but someone in the relationship has to yield. Someone has to not be petty and not act small by not returning fire with fire, in order for God to redeem or restore that relationship. We must move in grace.

Now, I am not suggesting that if you are consistently being kind to a spouse who is indifferent that the tables will turn in your favor and bring restoration. Chances are it might not get any better. Chances are your spouse could still pick up their things and walk out on your life, regardless of what you do to exhibit kindness to them. God has given each and every one of us the power of choice, the choice to choose between right and wrong, the choice to make good or extremely bad decisions which will have ramifications in our lives. At the end of the day, what I am suggesting is to choose to exhibit the same kindness to that insubordinate or unloving spouse anyway. By your willingness to show it anyway, not only does it build character in you, it sets you up for God's greatest breakthroughs and miracles in your life.

Principle 3: Show kindness, and watch God make the impossible possible.

God can and will restore the years the palmerworm and cankerworm and caterpillars have eaten from your life (Joel 2:25 KJV). Although it may have seemed like a waste of energy to be kind to someone who never acknowledged or appreciated it, God will repay you somehow, some way! If we believe in his infinite power and supreme authority, then we know that nothing is too hard for God. Yes, I believe he can restore a marriage relationship, regardless of how fragmented it might have become. If we do our part by exhibiting kindness and serving our spouse (even when there is no valid reason for doing so), God can shift that impossibility to something possible.

As I have stated earlier, kindness is not an emotion but an act. Regardless of how difficult it is to always be kind in a family relationship, a friendship, a marriage, or even a coworker scenario, you have the power to choose to change the dynamics of the relationship by being kind.

We have the opportunity to make an impact by showing that we are above the negativity and respond in kind ways, like:

- Giving the person our undivided attention when they are speaking.

- Not trying to interject our opinion but giving them room to speak.

- Being willing to be present in helping with a task, such as cleaning their home, doing the laundry, or running some errands.

- Calling them to see how they are doing.

"God demonstrates his own love for us in this: While we were still sinners, Christ died for us" (Romans 5:8). God sent Jesus Christ in the hope that mankind would receive Christ, but not all did. Matter of fact, even today many reject Jesus as God and won't acknowledge his kingship. God knew that some would and some wouldn't receive Christ, yet he displayed his love or act of kindness by sending mankind a lifeline through Jesus. If God acted in kindness, he expects us to do the same with others who are not easy to love.

We all have people in our lives who test us. Loving them is as difficult as climbing Mount Everest. It's painful and tough, but our job is to do it without ever expecting anything in return. When our expectations are low when showing kindness, then we reduce the ability to be hurt when people don't respond in kind.

Although your kindness might never be reciprocated on earth, God sees and knows your labors of love. You have shown love to the person who has been difficult to love, and in some way, God gave you the strength to carry out your moments of kindness.

Principle 4: Kindness is never about you.

One of the motivational statements my father, Donald Clarke, Sr., used—to rally the church to evangelize the city—was "We are serving a cause greater than ourselves." Serving is never about our self-interest. It is about being conscious of others around us, even the "difficult" people. The same could be said about kindness. What we do for others has a lasting impact that can change the course of their lives. We will talk more in detail about that later.

> *"That those who have trusted*
> *in God may be careful to*
> *devote themselves to doing*
> *what is good. These things are*
> *excellent and profitable for*
> *everyone."*
> —*Titus 3:7–9*

We have personal things going on in our lives that give us every right to be short, hostile, or abrupt with anyone we encounter. After all, we are not robots; we are human beings. However, placing the characteristic of kindness at the front, as our first response to others regardless of the circumstance, says we serve a cause greater than ourselves—God's love.

There will be seasons when you won't want to be kind. There will be moments in life when you are inundated with many difficult personal circumstances all happening at once, and the last thing you can possibly do is think of ways to help others too. We are all built with the internal desire to be self-centered, to look out for ourselves first before helping others. In these moments, the challenge is to dig deep within ourselves and go the extra mile to assist someone else as well rather than give full attention to our own problems. I'm not saying we should ignore our problems, but we must seek ways to help others with their problems as well. It is called seeing the bigger picture and asking God what to do about it.

In Galatians 5:22–23, the apostle Paul listed a few characteristics which indicate the fruit of the Spirit is in us, and guess what's there? You got it: kindness. Why would it be in the Canon if it wasn't important to God? One of the main features about us as believers—that would compel a world lost in sin and seeking hope and healing—is that we need to become God's walking, breathing, and living billboards of kindness. This will compel unbelievers to want to know more about the God we follow. Is it easy, especially when all hell is breaking out in our lives? Kids lose their natural minds, a spouse is acting like one of the kids, coworkers hate on us, the boss is testing us, bills are behind, parents are sick, and on and on. The task is to rise above all that because in life, there will always be trouble. That is the one thing we can't escape or run from. Even Jesus said "In this world you will have trouble. But take heart! I have overcome the world" (John 16:33). Jesus overcame, and that's a good sign we will too. In the meantime, Jesus would want us to demonstrate his love and do our best to weather the storms with grace.

We will never know who is observing our actions and judging us by our conduct. All the more reason we should maintain an even-keel calmness and a good attitude in showing kindness—someone could be watching, and our action could be the very message they need to not make permanent bad decisions based on temporary problems. There are countless stories of individuals who were going to commit suicide and end their pain of loneliness and depression when someone came along and showed them they cared. The act of kindness is life changing. If only we could understand its power to transform lives.

CHAPTER 4

THE PARALLEL BETWEEN KINDNESS AND PERSONAL GROWTH

*Whoever pursues
righteousness and love
. . . finds life, prosperity and
honor.*
—Proverbs 21:21

You never know what you can do until you actually do it. To be kind is not just a Christian principle of being a disciple of Christ, it also directly impacts personal growth in your life.

First and foremost, it takes maturity to be kind to others who have been hostile to you. The act of kindness is a matter of the heart and mind. When the mind is transformed by the truth of God's Word, it shifts our perspective on how we respond to life, people, and circumstances.

When the apostle Paul said "Do not be conformed to this world, but be transformed by the renewal of your mind" (Romans 12:2 ESV), he was alluding to the fact that when we encounter the Word of God on a daily and continual basis and apply it, the impact of a renewed mind will dictate how we think and respond in every season in life.

Be Whole and Free

Our predisposition is to hold grudges and not be cordial or nice to others when we are done wrong. It is only a part of human nature to respond in that manner. It is much easier to have some animosity toward people who have abused, misused, molested, falsely accused, or berated us. We have every right to feel that way, but there is a better way. When we ingest the truth of the Word of God and allow his Holy Spirit to heal us from the wounds of yesterday, he gives us the strength and grace to forgive and go the extra mile of being kind to the offender, when there is no reason to at all. Now this could take time, and in most cases it does. Healing from emotional scars takes time. Forgiveness is required to release them so you can live. I advise you to seek a professional counselor who can walk you through that process. The key thing is to take your time. Allow God to heal you through whatever method works so you can be whole and free.

I've heard it said that forgiveness is never about the offender but is about you getting freed from the prison of the past. Your ability to be kind in adverse situations, even in the face of the person who committed the hurtful act against you, can calmly show them the grace of God. To extend help is a great indicator of personal growth. To do the antithesis of that and be hostile, aggressive, and cold toward the person only shows there is more room to grow in forgiveness, and more room to learn and grow in God.

To be kind doesn't make hurtful experiences easier. Matter of fact, being kind can sometimes be the greatest challenge you'll ever have to experience in your life, but showing kindness will yield great growth. It will give you a new perspective of yourself in the present versus who you were yesterday. You'll create your own new reality. Choose to lead your life and grow (not go) into who you would like to become.

The Growth Kindness Brings

As I stated before, it takes a mature, healed, and stable person to show kindness when he or she has been taken advantage of by others. It will be the greatest and probably the most difficult thing you and I will have to do in this life. I say "have to" because to be kind is also a kingdom prerequisite in loving God.

In Matthew 22, we read about how Jesus shared with his disciples a Mosaic law about loving God. He said "'You shall love the Lord your God with all your heart, with all your soul, and with all your mind.' This is the first and great commandment. And the second is like it: 'You shall love your neighbor as yourself'" (vv. 37–39 NKJV). Please note there was never a condition to loving the neighbor. No neighbor has to love us back, but the requirement of us is love.

In some way, I feel Jesus was telling his disciples then, and readers today, to reach beyond the feelings and expectations of receiving anything in return, and to love the ones who are most difficult to love—in the same way my father did for everyone he met. God did this without any reservations. He loved us by sending his Son as the atonement of our sin, for the sake of saving humankind.

For us to love our neighbors, it is more about the principle of dying to oneself and one's desires, even though it may not be reciprocated. I believe the moment we can become "dead" to what someone might or might not do in return is the moment we experience spiritual growth in God. This kind of growth can't be found cruising through life on easy street, where everything that can go well is happening. Money is aplenty, kids are fed, relationships are good; we have no debts, no creditors calling to collect, and all is peaches and cream. We would all love that. But character is built under duress. Stress stretches us to places we thought we could never be stretched, and circumstances teach more about life than can be found in any book.

"Count it all joy when you fall into various trials, knowing that the testing of your faith produces patience. But let patience have its perfect work, that you may be perfect and complete, lacking nothing."
—James 1:1–2 NKJV

The ability not to be moved by emotions triggered by what others do or don't do indicates that we have matured past the place of needing others to positively respond in order to act kindly toward them. Difficult people—whether family, friends, or foes—teach us more about how we can love like Jesus did. He selflessly gave his life for humanity, becoming the ultimate sacrifice for the sins of the world! If that isn't love, then we have to ask what is. This is the greatest single act of any kindness. It transcends cultural barriers and socioeconomic classes and reaches to the heart of man. We are charged with the same challenge to love, without stipulation or reservations, being the example Jesus was on earth.

Kindness Has Additional Benefits

It has been scientifically proven that the act of kindness has physiological, emotional, and mental effects on the body of the giver! Kindness doubles when we share with others. Studies have shown that if we can share one act of kindness a day, it will start a ripple effect on the body of a reduction in stress and anxiety and an improved mood—which makes one feel calmer, healthier, and happier. The serotonin kindness produces in our brain makes us feel happier and releases endorphins which reduce pain and increase energy. We get to be just as blessed as those we are kind to.

I used the term "kill them with kindness." Now I hope you know I am not actually telling you to kill them while you smile . . . alright? That is not the advice I'm giving. I am suggesting you be willing to go the extra mile in showing acts of kindness to someone. It's hard then to sit back and wait or watch for the effect of your kindness. It won't take long before they ask you, "Why are you doing this for me? I treated you wrong yet you are so cordial to me. You were willing to help me even though I never extended my help to you."

This will be an opportunity and moment for healing and reconciliation in your relationship, all stemming from the willingness to be kind.

The Proven Results of Kindness

Eric Swanson, adjunct professor at Denver Seminary, tells this story:

> I surveyed my church to see if people saw a relationship between ministering to others and spiritual growth. When asked, "To what extent has your ministry or service to others affected your spiritual growth?"
>
> - 92 percent answered positively. None responded that ministry had a negative effect on their spiritual growth.
>
> - 63 percent indicated that service was equally significant in their spiritual growth compared to other spiritual disciplines, such as Bible study and prayer.
>
> - 24 percent responded that ministry or service to others had been "a more significant factor"

> to their spiritual growth than Bible study or prayer.
>
> - Over half (58 percent) of those who were not actively ministering to others felt either "not satisfied" or "somewhat satisfied" with their level of spiritual growth.
>
> —Eric Swanson, "What You Get from Giving." (Leadership Journal, Spring 2003), p. 37.

One of the blessings of showing kindness to others is that we get to grow deeper in our relationship with God because we're doing things his way and seeing others his way. We're living in love more. The apostle Paul made kindness a staple of his ministry for a reason, and he left us with this charge: "You yourselves know that these hands of mine have supplied my own needs and the needs of my companions. In everything I did, I showed you that by this kind of hard work we must help the weak, remembering the words the Lord Jesus himself said: 'It is more blessed to give than to receive'" (Acts 20:34–35). Let's follow his example.

CHAPTER 5

KINDNESS AND LEGACY

A life is not important except in the impact it has on other lives.
—Jackie Robinson

Like Paul, we will all leave an imprint in this life. Positively or negatively, how we live our lives will be the determining factor in how we are remembered in the annals of time. What I have discovered is that if we want to be successful and have the courage to step into the unknown or do what has never been done, we must live life intentionally.

Living life intentionally means we will experience low and high moments. The skies won't always be blue. We will experience gloomy or even stormy seasons such as family issues, financial restrictions, or job losses, when it will feel like the easiest thing would be to throw in the towel. That's the moment we keep on moving forward and pressing ahead, in spite of the disappointments and painful times. We stay the course.

The Legacy Impact of Kindness

Donald Clarke, Sr. has an incredible story of the long-term results of one act of kindness:

> In my senior year at Glenmuir High School, I had to temporarily drop out because one of my shoes lost its sole. I was in despair until two students from school showed up at my house saying that Dr. Sydney Scott, the school's principal, had missed me from school and was concerned about my well-being. I conveyed to them my predicament, which they conveyed to Dr. Scott, who promptly summoned me to his office the next day. He gave me a sealed letter and instructed me to take it to the manager of the Bata Shoe store in May Pen.

Upon delivering the letter, the manager measured my feet and then presented me with a gleaming pair of brown leather shoes. The next day I was back in class at Glenmuir studying for my General Certificate of Education (GCE) examinations administered by the University of Cambridge in London, England. When the results came out, I had successfully passed:

- English with distinction
- English Literature with distinction
- Biology with distinction
- Bible Knowledge with distinction

Before I even got my GCE results, Dr. Scott called his friend Mr. Burrell, the head of Mid-Clarendon Irrigation, a part of the Ministry of Agriculture, and asked him to hire me as the youngest paymaster at that agency. Dr. Scott's acts of kindness to me helped change the trajectory of my life forever, and it is today impacting thousands globally. He was simply incredible.

> Because of this, the church where I serve, Harvest Fire—the best church on the planet, may I say—started a Pay It Forward campaign. In this campaign we encouraged our members to show an act of kindness to someone who never expected it.

Through my father's global church and religious outreaches, we have won thousands for Christ on four continents, cared for the homeless and undernourished in the Miami area, and brought help to the helpless in places as far away as India.

In the secular space, he has taught for the likes of General Electric Capital in places like the UK, US, India, and China—having global influence in the corporate finance space. He sat on the faculty of the Secured Finance Network, having taught for them for over thirty years. He has assisted such lenders as RBS Global and the National Bank of Ireland build asset-based lending platforms, and he has written the globally acclaimed book *Asset Based Lending Disciplines,* published in 2006 by The Commercial Finance Association.

How did he get here? One principal of an Anglican-based high school, Glenmuir

High School in May Pen, Clarendon, Jamaica, showed him acts of kindness. Like the Good Samaritan in the Scriptures, he rescued my father from a life destined to fail and launched him into his destiny. As he puts it, "Dr. Sydney H. Scott, my angel, now celebrates the joys of heaven."

Pay It Forward

The one thing our church is big on is meeting the needs of the people. My father believed that we could not reach the hearts of the people unless we were able to meet most of their urgent needs. Now, we do not have robust social programs. As a matter of fact, most of the ventures we take on are done on a shoestring budget with very little outside assistance. Yet we run a food bank, where we feed over six hundred families bi-weekly; we have a housing assistance program for men and women needing a hand up in society; and we run events where we give free gas to our community.

Caring for the needs of people is at the heart of God. We have found that people are attracted to those who not only express empathy but who help where help is needed. Actions truly speak louder than words. Stan Toler, in his book *The Power of Influence,* said "Influence is a gradual force. It seems like nothing is happening, but the impact is felt over time." In order to make an impact, we must be willing to express kindness to others, which I believe will distinguish us from others who ignore the needs around them.

Kindness Changes Our Legacy

My mother, Helga Clarke (the smartest woman I know), told me there is always someone in the world who has it worse than you. What may seem like a big deal in our context is miniscule in another person's situation. When we are able to reach beyond ourselves by doing acts of kindness, we can leave a lasting legacy on the hearts and mind of people we touch. We can do things like serve at the local food bank, help people buy groceries for their families, volunteer time to be a big brother or sister to children without parents in their lives, or give up weekends to cut lawns for the elderly. That's what I call living life intentionally. It's having the ability to take the focus off of yourself and relieve someone else's burden with your act of kindness. Now, I do believe there should be a balanced approach to all of this. You can't possibly attend to the needs of others in your sphere and forget about your family's needs or your personal needs. However, I do believe wholeheartedly that we can step out of our world of concern to be kind to others. It's a matter of shifting the focus off ourselves and coming to the aid of someone else. This could change our perspective on life.

When you can help someone else, it gives you a sense of pride to have served a cause greater than yourself. Lonely people are people who just tend to their own affairs, never helping others or giving them a hand up in life.

Kindness Breeds Success

My father once said that the greatness of a man should never be measured by the house he lives in, the car he drives, or the wealth he has amassed at the pinnacle of his life but rather by how many fellow men he has taken with him in his ascent to the top. Success begins with the seeds of hope we deposit in the lives of others.

Jesus painted a story of this—about a good Samaritan who stopped to help a man who was robbed, beaten, and left for dead on the side of the Jerusalem to Jericho road (Luke 10:25–37). As this man lay clinging to life, hoping someone would help, a priest saw him, ignored him, and kept on walking. A Levite observed this man lying there, in need of attention and help, yet he too walked by without offering assistance. A Samaritan passed by. In that time, Samaritans were considered unclean people. Jews did not hang out with these gentiles—people outside the Jewish bloodline—and they looked down on them. Yet it was the Samaritan who saw this desperate man clinging to life and was willing to stop whatever he had going on in his personal agenda, put oil on the man's wounds, put him on his donkey, bring him to the nearest inn, and pay for his stay for a few days until he got better. To Jesus, the Samaritan was more of a superstar than the priest and the Levite. Both claimed to know God but wouldn't show love for a stranger via a simple act of kindness.

As mentioned earlier, Jesus said the greatest among us are the ones who serve. Service requires us to place our own list of things to do aside and focus on helping those who need us. It demands we go the extra the mile to help elevate someone from their current circumstances. It teaches us humility as we extend ourselves to our fellow men.

Mother Teresa was born on August 26, 1910, in Skopje, the capital of the Republic of Macedonia. Even as a little girl, she felt the call to serve as a nun through helping the poor. At the age of eighteen, she went to Ireland to learn English at a convent, and after her training, she went to India, where she took her formal religious vows in service as a nun.

She was working as a teacher in Calcutta, India, for twenty years when she was called to help the poor of India. She had little support while she was attempting to feed the poorest of the poor, and she was often hungry herself. She continued to carry out this missionary task by developing a group called the Missionaries of Charity. The goal was to take care of the destitute, the naked, the uncared for and dejected of society by offering them hope and practical help.

Mother Teresa continued this noteworthy cause until her death. Her willingness to show kindness and serve a cause greater than herself brought her recognition—from having an airport named after her to being awarded the Nobel Peace Prize in 1979 and awarded an honorary US citizenship in 1996. She is still remembered to this very day for her heart in exhibiting kindness to others and her sacrifices of love.

The act of kindness has a lasting impact that places us in the arena of the greats. We will never be forgotten because of our willingness to help others in need.

Kindness Is about Serving in Humility

Service is the action of helping or doing work for someone. It is mainly the action of setting aside one's own agenda for a moment to assist the needs of others.

To exhibit kindness is to have the ability to serve. Unfortunately, service doesn't get much attention, notoriety, or popularity today, therefore, many don't volunteer their time to serve but look to be served!

Jesus told his disciples, "The greatest among you should be like the youngest, and the one who rules like the one who serves" (Luke 22:26). This statement came at the same hour Jesus would be betrayed by his very own. He was preparing his disciples, whom he had been with for three years, for his death. He told them that one of them would betray him, and the next thing that transpired was a heated discussion among the disciples as to who that person was. The discussion moved from interrogating each other to figuring out who was the greatest among them! Go figure! Jesus was about to die in a few hours, he was trying to have an intimate moment with his disciples, and in the middle of what was a crisis, the disciples began a kindergarten fight as to who was the greatest? You can't make this stuff up!

Jesus shared, "The kings of the Gentiles lord it over them; and those who exercise authority over them call themselves Benefactors. But you are not to be like that" (Luke 22:25–26). Jesus was indicating to the disciples that it's not about importance or titles that will get the attention of God, it is our service. That places us at the top of the totem pole with him.

When we become consumer minded, caught in the frenzy of pursuing products and services for personal gain, always looking for ways to be served rather than to serve, we lose the greatest opportunity to leave an imprint in the lives of others—offering kind acts to those in need.

> He has shown you, O mortal, what is good.
> And what does the LORD require of you?
> To act justly and to love mercy
> and to walk humbly with your God.
> —Micah 6:8

Service, to some extent, hinges on the very willingness to be kind by offering ourselves to others. The world needs leaders who are not just considered successful by what they have accomplished or the accolades they have received; the world needs servant leaders—people who are willing to go the extra mile to encourage, uplift, or support someone else. That is leaving a legacy. That is making an impact!

CHAPTER 6

LET KINDNESS TAKE THE LEAD

*As we have opportunity, let us
do good to all people.
—Galatians 6:10*

Each day we are gifted by God to maximize the moments of our lives and make a significant impact, and it all boils down to choices we make. We are the total sum of the choices we make, negative or positive. The decisions we make on this planet called earth will either forge our name in history for love or make us infamous for the unloving acts we have done.

Whether you believe in God or not, it is quoted in the Scriptures that each and every one of us will give an account to God at the end of our life. If we squandered time being selfish, petty, or insubordinate to the awareness of God, living life on our own terms, that's what we'll be judged on. Or we could live life purposefully, loving and serving God and serving others. We have to choose to let kindness take the lead and discover a newfound satisfaction in serving a cause greater than ourselves. We've learned by now that kindness is a kingdom principle, a mandate for believers in Christ to exhibit in our daily lives.

Kindness as a Way of Life

Now you may say, "Don, I get the point. It's clear! But what do you mean when you say to let kindness take the lead?" Well, I am glad you asked. Let me show you how.

Since we are a sum total of the decisions we make, let me give you three simple ways we can let kindness take the lead.

1. **Choose to live selflessly instead of selfishly each day!**

My favorite author of the New Testament, the apostle Paul, put it this way: "Do nothing from selfishness or empty conceit [through factional motives, or strife], but with [an attitude of] humility [being neither arrogant nor self-righteous], regard others as more important than yourselves" (Philippians 2:3 AMP).

One way to slay selfishness and become more kind is to become more aware of others' needs rather than your own. The problems in the political arena in comparison to those in a regular household are that in our own house, we get so consumed with what we can do to better our lives and those attached to us that we don't spend any time thinking of ways to help others. If we declared each day, "I am going to make a sacrifice and make a difference in someone's life today!" we would definitely shift our natural construct of self-awareness to people awareness.

Jesus mastered this skill of people awareness. We may have a need of our own while we show kindness to others; however, I do believe that in some way, God can and will open a flood of miracle provision for us as we sacrificially extend ourselves in kindness.

2. Choose to be thoughtful.

It costs nothing to be nice. Absolutely nothing. I believe it takes more effort to be stingy and mean-spirited. Maybe that's just me. At times, all it takes is giving a compliment to someone to lift their mood, or writing them a nice note to share how much you appreciate them. This could mean a world of difference.

We never know what people are going through each day. Although some people carry their burdens with a smile, it doesn't mean it's easy. A simple gesture could go a long way and have a lasting effect on the recipient. Life is hard, and we all need someone to express their care when we're going through a tough time. There is no better way to show kindness than to be thoughtful in word and deed whenever possible.

3. Choose to be present.

We live in a culture that prioritizes the hustle of making life better, setting goals, and overworking to achieve those goals— so much so that we forget to live in the moment for our families and friends, or for the people around us. I believe being present is special, and it demonstrates kindness beautifully. Jesus showed this attribute very well, not only with his disciples, whom he spent three years with, but with the people around him who needed healing or deliverance from bondage.

I had to learn to not be so mentally distracted. I was moving fast, thinking one thousand miles per hour, and I wasn't able to stand still to listen to others' experiences or be present in our conversations, even when they needed my attention in the moment! John Maxwell said it best in his blog post "The Greatest Sign of Conflict and How to Address It": "Learn to walk slowly through the crowd." This simply means we should take the time to be sensitive to others' concerns—whether it's your spouse, child, or family member talking. Slow down to hear their thoughts. I am learning this principle with my son Elijah. I'm choosing to sit and listen to his latest commentary on the *Legends of Korra* show or *Dragon Ball Z!* He can be very passionate about it, and if I don't give him my undivided attention, he won't stop until he knows I've heard every blow-by-blow account of what has happened in the show. These are moments

I'll never get back, so I am being intentional about not wasting them and being present for him.

As a pastor, I had to learn that the people are my focus when I am physically present in church. They need their pastor's advice and sound counsel, and my mind must be free of distractions to hear their pain, even express empathy for it, and offer hope via Jesus Christ! It is my mandate and my call to do so, but not just with the people God has so kindly awarded me to shepherd. I must be present for any others I may be in contact with outside the realm of ministry.

Kindness is predicated on our ability to be present. This translates to, "I am here and you have my undivided attention." Kindness requires a heart of compassion to help someone in need, even if it is just taking the time to sit and be a listening ear to someone's pain.

Two friends of mine, Eddy Gervais and Daniel Rios, showed me this kindness when I went through my divorce—one of the most traumatic experience of my life. These two brothers came to my home to hang with me till the wee hours of morning. They always took my incoming calls and sacrificed countless hours listening to me as I poured my pain on them. They offered counsel each and every time I got stuck in a rut I couldn't get myself out of, and the time they invested in me was and is priceless. No amount of money could buy what those guys did for me, and for that I am sincerely indebted to them!

Kindness shouldn't be rare. It shouldn't get lost because of our complex, busy calendars that are loaded with so many things to do that we forget to be human and forget to take time to be present for others.

All it takes to lead with kindness is effort! All it takes is having a compassionate heart.

CHAPTER 7

THE NEED FOR MORE CIVILITY

Aspire to decency. Practice civility toward one another. Admire and emulate ethical behavior wherever you find it. Apply a rigid standard of morality to your lives; and if, periodically, you fail—as you surely will—adjust your lives, not the standards."
—Ted Koppel

One thing I quickly discovered about life is that no man is an island. There will come a point in time where we all will need a shoulder to cry on, a person to listen, someone to care enough to be present in our times of distress. Honestly, life can get lonely when you are facing insurmountable challenges. Problems have a tendency to make us feel alone, like our situation is an isolated incident and no one else could possibly be going through what we are going through. The truth is someone on this planet *is* going through what you are going through, and probably worse. There is always a need to be hospitable and kindhearted to others, because we never know what is transpiring in someone's life.

The reason I titled this last chapter "The Need for More Civility" is for the fact that in our culture, all the differences—on political views, faith dogmas or ideals, ethnic backgrounds, and upbringing—can place us at odds with each other at times. One thing the protest over the unjust killing of George Floyd taught me is that despite our heated political and cultural differences, people can come together, even in the middle of a pandemic, for a greater cause.

It shouldn't take an incident such as unjust policing or an act of inequality to prompt us to show kindness in the form of unity or solidarity. Kindness should exude from our hearts with the thought of how we can influence, impact, transform, or change someone's life for the better. We live in a new generation where, if there are differences in opinion or a misunderstanding of some kind, the new trend is to "cancel" or socially exile the person with the different opinion. This is wrong! This act of cruelty is not a part of God's kingdom.

Jesus taught many things on forgiveness, but the main scripture that sticks out to me is "If you do not forgive others their sins, your Father will not forgive your sins" (Matthew 6:15). While this new generation is big on the social cancellation of others, where would mankind be, I wonder, if Christ canceled us? I will tell you: We'd be doomed to an eternal hell, without hope, needing salvation, and with no direct connection to the Father. Cancel culture is hostile to God because it is not a part of his kingdom culture. Believers, especially, need to demonstrate the love of Jesus to others. He was patient with us even when we were reborn in him with our imperfections and, at times, willful sins—the times we turned our backs and abandoned him until we came to our senses and recognized our need for him.

Showing Kindness Beyond Mistakes

God is like the father of the prodigal son who wanted his inheritance while his father was still alive, to live life the way he saw fit (Luke 15:11–32). The request of the prodigal son was dishonorable and disrespectful because sons back then would only get their inheritance after the death of a parent or guardian. For him to ask while his father was still alive was like a slap in the face to the father. Although it was painful, the father gave the son his inheritance and the son left for his journey to freedom. Jesus shared in this parable how this son squandered all his resources and money to the point of abject poverty, where it left him begging others just to survive. Things got even worse: when no one would give him anything, he resorted to eating the carob pods the pigs ate to live.

Sin will always over promise and under deliver. That's a message for another book. One day the son was eating with the pigs when he came to his senses and realized he didn't have to live the way he was living. He knew he could go back home to his father and ask for forgiveness and his father would take him in. This son gathered himself and began the journey home. He was probably tired, hungry, and embarrassed about the decisions he had made, all while limping on the road back home to his dad. The father saw a man on the road walking toward his house. As the man got closer, the father realized that it was his son who had left and had come back. The Bible states that while he was still a far way off, the father ran down the road to meet him and embrace him. The father shouted, "Quickly bring out the best robe [for the guest of honor] and put it on him; and give him a ring for his hand, and sandals for his feet. And bring the fattened calf and slaughter it, and let us [invite everyone and] feast and celebrate; for this son of mine was [as good as] dead and is alive again; he was lost and has been found" (Luke 15:22–24 AMP). He celebrated for the mere fact that his son was home. No matter how far he had gone or what he had done, the son would always be welcomed back home.

One thing I love about Christ is that his arms are always open, ready to take us in, no matter what sin or crime we have committed or who we have committed it with. He stands on call to love us beyond our conditional state and to restore and deliver us from our plight.

I am really convinced that if we could exhibit this kind of kindness, compassion, and extended mercy to each other despite the mistakes made, it would transform our world as we know it for the better. It would become heaven on earth if we all could demonstrate this level of forgiveness and kindness instead of hostility!

Final Thoughts

IT COSTS ABSOLUTELY NOTHING to be kind. Kindness can't be taught; however, I do believe it can be practiced. If we all could practice ways of thinking outside our context and discovering ways to help others around us, the effects of this expression could last through history. It all begins in the heart. What are we willing to sacrifice to make someone less fortunate comfortable? What are we willing to do to ensure a family doesn't have their power shut off, to be a friend to a lonely senior at a nursing home, or to offer groceries to a single mother struggling to keep her children fed? It's not about the act but more about the heart and our willingness to serve someone else and not cater to our own needs. Think about it. Serving others is not a natural thing to do; however, when we do serve, it teaches us how to be more in tune, aware, and sensitive to the needs of those we serve. We cannot be kind without serving.

I believe we have the remedy to change the world. We can change a generation by spreading kindness, by spreading love to others the way God did through what his Son Jesus Christ did, offering his life for humanity. This was the ultimate sacrificial demonstration of kindness and it is kindness personified.

Kindness is choosing daily to make the sacrifice, to go the extra mile, to think of others above yourself and do what you can to make someone's day better. It all boils down to being kind.

About the Author

Coupled with a love for God's people, Pastor Donald F. Clarke, Jr. has a tremendous passion for the Word of God. Since childhood, Pastor Don has always felt the call of God upon his life and has had a heart for ministering the gospel of Jesus Christ. At the mere age of six years old, he boldly announced to his mother, "I want to preach like my father and sing like Jimmy Swaggart!" And that is exactly what he did and what he continues to do today.

Under the leadership of his father and mother, Bishop Dr. Donald and Pastor Dr. Helga Clarke, Pastor Don began his ministry as the youth pastor of Harvest Fire Worship Center's "Joshua Generation." During his eight-year tenure as youth pastor, God used him mightily to build a powerful and vibrant youth ministry that heavily impacted and ignited the lives of many teenagers and young adults.

Currently serving as the lead pastor of Harvest Fire Worship Center, Pastor Don's focus is faith, family, and future. Under the guidance of the Holy Spirit and support of the Harvest Fire leadership team, Pastor Don's heart is to solidify the faith, strengthen family systems, and secure the future of believers. Pastor Don ministers extensively throughout the United States and also internationally.

Pastor Don is also a songwriter and author. He has written a book entitled *The Thankful Life* that and cowritten a hit single "Livin' Clean" with two-time Grammy nominee Canton Jones. Pastor Don received his associate degree in arts from Broward Community College, a bachelor's degree in business from the American Intercontinental University, and a master of arts in biblical studies from South Florida Bible College & Theological Seminary.

He is the proud father of one son, Elijah Peter Clarke.

Harvest Fire

Harvest Fire Worship Center, Inc./Harvest
Fire International Outreach
18291 NW 23rd Avenue
Miami Gardens, Florida 33056
(305) 620-2986
www.harvestfireworshipcenter.com

Social Media

Instagram:
www.instagram.com/donclarkejr

Facebook:
www.facebook.com/profile.php?id=100000
324340950